Paperback ISBN: 978-1-7338666-6-8

Publisher: Gloria J. Rayborn

Scripture quotations are primarily from the King James Version of the Bible.

PRINTED IN THE UNITED STATES OF AMERICA

Dedication

This book is dedicated to my late parents - Willie Lee and Essie Lee Brown - and the very large family that they were faithful to bring into the world and nurture, protect, and develop. I appreciate now, more than ever, the many sacrifices they made in order to help us survive and thrive. A special dedication to those loved ones – my sister, niece, aunts, uncles, cousins, brother-in-law, and grandparents - who have also transitioned into eternity. I love you all and thank God for blessing me with you.

I dedicate my poem, "There is a Place", to each of you.

There is a place I long to go
It's way up in the heavens - or so I've been told.
In that city there are streets paved with gold.
No misery, no poverty, no strife, no death there.
Love fills the city and there's joy everywhere.
No sickness, no crying, no hurting there;
No smog, no pollution, no viruses in the air.

How can I get there, some people may ask?
Can I buy my way in or complete a big task?
Can I travel by bus, by car, or by train?
Do I take the subway or fly on an airplane?
No, was the answer to each question asked.
You can't buy your way in or complete a big task.
No bus, car, train, subway or airplane will take you there.
You can't buy a ticket or pay a fare.

There is only one way to get to live in that city.
Accept that Jesus Christ died a brutal death on the cross

Out of love and not out of pity.
He died on the cross to pay the price for our sins,
And three days later He rose again.

He showed himself to those who had followed Him,
And explained God's plan of salvation to each one of them.
He gave them instructions on what to do
So that those who believe and accept Him would live for eternity,
too.

One day He's coming back to claim His own
And take those who love Him to their new home.
There is no way to the Father but through Jesus His Son,
He's fought the sin battle and already won!

No crying, no dying, no hurt, no fear, no tears there.
No lying, no evil will be found anywhere.
God's love fills the city. There is love, peace and joy everywhere
Forever free from heartache and harm
As you stay in His presence and rest in His arms!

Other books written by Gloria Rayborn include:

"I Am Special"

"Sharing"

"Let's Go On a Treasure Hunt: Searching for Hidden Treasure"

"Handing Down A Legacy Of Blessings: Things I Want You to Know What I Hope You Will Be & Things I Hope You Will Do"

TABLE OF CONTENTS

Foundation For A Legacy of Blessings
Good Seeds Planted by My Sharecropper Family

Introduction

During this pause related to Covid19 and the ensuing "social and physical distancing" that has occurred, I've had plenty of time to reflect on how life has changed over these past few months. Death, sickness, disease, loneliness, economic changes, protests, and even changes in how we worship have been part of this pause.

Not all changes have been bad. This time has allowed some of us to spend more time with family, more time to relax and catch up on chores, time for self-reflection and more time to spend with God.

This book is an outcome of that time of self-reflection. I've been remembering the ones we've lost - before and during Covid19 - and how our lives today have been guided and influenced by seeds that were planted years ago by my family. The focus of this book is only on the good seeds that were planted. Not everything in my life was perfect, and not every seed planted was good, but I have chosen to focus on the positives and the lessons learned from those things. It's been said that "hindsight is always 20/20". Well, I wish I understood then what I understand now.

I don't remember my childhood in a lot of detail, but more than six decades later, there are some things that still stand out. Those memories and lessons learned are the things that are included in this book which focuses on the seeds of: family, knowledge & wisdom, faith, and legacy. Those early learnings were also the foundation on which my book "*Handing Down A Legacy of Blessings*" was based.

PART I: SEEDS OF FAMILY

Family Life

I am the middle child of nine children – seven girls and two boys - born in a rural town in Mississippi to parents who were farmers. More specifically, for many years they were sharecroppers. Sharecroppers were tenant farmers who lived on farms. They were provided credit for things like seed and tools while they lived in houses provided by the landowner. They worked the land and received a share of the value of the crops produced minus any charges that had been made throughout the year. At some point, the arrangement changed from sharecropping to being paid as day laborers.

Everyone in our neighborhood had similar sharecropping arrangements. They worked long, hot, hard days in order to provide for their families. Children also helped to work the land. We began working in the fields chopping and picking cotton at a very early age. I remember being in the fields when I was around eight or nine years old. Despite the long hot work days, we children learned to make the days pass quickly by talking and challenging each other to finish chopping a row faster. Even after working hard all day, we still had energy left to play.

Neither of my parents graduated from high school. My dad told us that he had to quit high school after his father died so that he could help take care of his mom and his twin sister. His older brothers had already moved away from home, so he became the "man" of the house. My mother's mom died when she was young, and I believe she stopped school after the 7th grade. Although they didn't finish their education, the focus in our home from an early age was for us children to get an education, work hard, take care of family, be responsible, and have faith in God.

Family was always important. The majority of our neighbors were relatives – uncles, aunts, and cousins. I only got to meet one of my grandparents because the others had all died before I was born. We called my mother's dad, Papa. Papa loved people. He loved to walk and also loved to sing. The song I remember him singing quite often was, "I Will Trust in the Lord." Papa lived a long life and died after I graduated from college.

Early in life, I never realized that I was poor because we always had what we needed. Everyone around us had the same or similar things as we had; similar houses – wood houses with tin roofs, a front porch, a wood or coal burning black stove, no air conditioning nor central heat. Fans were used to circulate the hot air and a stove provided heat.   Initially there was no indoor plumbing. We heated bath water on the stove and took baths in a tin tub.   Of course, no indoor plumbing meant that we had to use an outhouse. We pumped water using an outdoor pump and when that water was no longer drinkable, we hauled water from a well that was several miles away. We cleaned our clothes using either a scrub board and tub or a washing machine that had a wringer. Clotheslines were used to dry our clothes. Sometimes the lines were made with barbed wire. Mattresses and pillows were homemade and stuffed with cotton.

We shared what we had with each other and looked out for each other. Our best friends were usually our cousins. We laughed, played, worked, worshipped, went to school, and got into trouble together.

There were no fancy birthday or Christmas gifts. I only remember getting one doll. I do recall a wagon and a bicycle that we shared and took turns playing with. We grew to expect a giant peppermint stick from Papa for Christmas. Our parents also bought boxes of Washington red delicious apples, oranges, and different kinds of nuts for the holidays. Pecan trees grew in the neighborhood and Mom would also use pecans on her caramel cakes.

We were ecstatic when we got our first Christmas tree. It was shiny and I think it was made out of tinsel. It came with a multicolor rotating light wheel that appeared to change the color of the tree as the wheel rotated. We kept that artificial tree for years.

Our original home only had five rooms. The living room also doubled as a bedroom with two beds that the children shared. We had a kitchen, a room that was used for storage and two more bedrooms. Our front porch had a swing that we loved. Our washer was set up on the front porch so that we could do laundry outside.

During the winter, extra things had to be done to keep us warm. The original house we were in was cold and drafty. My parents would place cotton in the cracks and crevices around the doors and around the windows to keep out the cold in order to keep us warm. All of us, who were old enough, were taught how to chop wood or gather coal for the fire. We were also taught how to start a fire and to keep it going.

Our parents didn't wait for winter to arrive to prepare for it. Throughout the year, we would see my mom and sometimes my aunts hand stitching quilts that would be used to keep us warm in the winter. They also gathered foods from the garden during the summer and canned them for use in the winter.

Our entertainment consisted of a black and white television, a radio, and a record player. The news and weather were watched daily; soap operas were watched during the week. We children were the remote control because we had to physically turn the television's knob in order to change channels. At midnight, the television stations played the Star Spangled Banner and then broadcasting ended. I remember watching two things that later impacted my life: a special Billy Graham Crusade that came on for several nights, and I watched men's college basketball with my oldest brother. We gravitated to two teams: UCLA and Memphis State. Today, I love the gospel of Jesus Christ. I played basketball in junior high and high school and have rekindled my love for watching basketball.

We primarily listened to music on the radio, and sometimes my relatives listened to baseball games. Every now and then, we were able to afford a record or an album that we sang and danced to.

Sometime during my late elementary or early junior high school days, we moved to a nicer house just across the road from our original house. We had indoor plumbing and propane gas heaters in some of the rooms. We were excited about the upgrades. Later we were able to have a window air conditioner for use in the summers.

Family Sticks Together

With nine children in the house, there were times when some of us would get into fights with each other. We usually got spanked for it and were told to hug and make up. Daddy always told us that we shouldn't fight each other and that we shouldn't start fights. However, if someone started a fight, it was our responsibility to fight back, and our siblings were to help because family sticks together.

We were disciplined when we did wrong; but our parents loved us and helped us whenever and however they could. Their goal was to keep us on the right path.

There was a family who rode the school bus with us that disliked our families. I never understood why they didn't like us, and there were frequent fights on the bus. I remember one time as I was getting off the bus someone pushed me from behind and caused me to fall into the mud. I was wearing my new maxi coat, which I loved. I was in elementary school and hadn't done anything. I started to cry. Well, a few of my cousins were still on the bus and they saw what happened. They then tackled the older high school girl who had pushed me off the bus. That girl was part of the family that hated our families. She never bothered me again.

Our parents were proud of our accomplishments. They made it a point to attend graduations – high school and college. They were also there for our weddings and helped with the grandchildren. We were appreciative of their support.

Another way our family stuck together was in how they helped to care for each other. When my uncle died, daddy stepped in to help my aunt take care of her nine children. I saw my grandfather, my aunt and cousins take care of one of my great aunts. I'm not sure what her illness was, but they cared for her until she died.

When my mom was diagnosed with Alzheimer's, daddy made the decision to be her caregiver for as long as he could. He was determined that she wouldn't be put in a nursing home. He kept that promise until she died. Thirty days later, he died.

Although family members won't always agree on every single item, that shouldn't prohibit them from loving each other and doing what they can to help one another. A house divided against itself shall not stand. Families should not let squabbles distract them from the true enemy. Family should always band together, fix what is broken, and move on in unity because there is power in unity.

PART II: SEEDS OF KNOWLEDGE & WISDOM

Waste Not, Want Not

When you don't have much, you learn to make the most with what you do have. Our parents never used being poor as an excuse. Rather, they learned to do what they could with what they had. Everyone worked – even the children. We had chores to do and also worked in the fields. Payment for our work - **$.50/hour** or **$5 for a 10 hour workday** - went to our parents who then used the money to help buy necessities for the family.

We were taught to not waste food. We had a garden consisting of tomatoes, different varieties of peas, butter beans, corn, okra, peanuts, onion, squash, watermelon, cantaloupes, greens – turnip, collard, cabbage, and mustard - and other food items. We spent time tending to the garden, harvesting the items and helping to prepare them for freezing or canning. Vegetables that we grew in the garden were a big part of our diet. We bought spaghetti, rice, grits, and pinto beans because they were cheap and could feed a lot of people. Corn bread, homemade biscuits, crackling bread were also part of our meals. Years later, corn flakes became a part of our diet.

We ate a lot of fried food because it was quicker to prepare. When we came home for lunch, we only had a short time to eat, to get a little bit of rest, and then return to the fields. We never went hungry. There was always something to eat and some meals were creative, but still good. There were times when buttermilk and cornbread sprinkled with sugar became a meal. Instead of peanut butter and jelly on bread, we sometimes had peanut butter on a biscuit with syrup. A favorite was grilled cheese on a piece of bread sprinkled with sugar. We also ate potted meat or Vienna sausages with saltine crackers, salmon croquettes with biscuits and syrup, sardines with hot sauce, and vanilla wafers with cheese.

Our protein sources included chicken (raised and store bought), pork – we raised our own hogs – some beef, and fish (catfish and buffalo fish). Periodically daddy would bring home a rabbit, turtle or deer that he had killed. Daddy bought the buffalo fish from a man who sold them out of his truck. My oldest brother had left home by then and my youngest brother was not old enough to help, so the girls had to clean the fish. None of us liked that job.

Every year my dad and uncles would kill several hogs. Each child had to help with either cleaning the chitterlings, pulling the hair from the hogs after they were doused in boiling water, or stirring the big black pots where the skins were cooked and lard was gathered from the hogs' fat. We also were responsible for grinding some of the meat into sausage. At one time, the meat was salted down and stored in a smoke house. In later years, rather than using the smoke house, the meat was wrapped, labeled and stored in the deep freezer. Every year when the hogs were slaughtered, our parents would send gifts of meat to others in the neighborhood.

When I was younger, we raised chickens and had a cow. We gathered eggs from the chicken coup, and also used the chickens as meat. We drank the milk and churned butter from the milk, and later also used the cow for meat.

Water and sweet tea were our primary drinks. Later, Kool-Aid became a favorite. Soft drinks and lunch meats were rare. We primarily had them during the holidays or when we had to buy food at the store because we couldn't go home for lunch when we worked as day laborers for other land owners.

Desserts were common in our household, but went into overdrive during the holidays. Common desserts were rice pudding, butter rolls, ice cream – sometimes homemade but later store bought - cakes (Rex Jelly, caramel with pecans, coconut, German chocolate, lemon and chocolate); sweet potato and lemon meringue pies; peach cobbler, fried apple fritters, tea cakes, and banana pudding. Momma made the best chicken and dressing – sometimes on Sundays and always for the holidays.

Be Resourceful

We were encouraged to only put food on our plates that we were going to eat. We had enough to eat, but not enough to waste. If we didn't eat all of our rice or biscuits, we would see those items reused for desserts. Rice became rice pudding and biscuits were made into bread pudding. Some of the husk from the corn was later used to make tea to assist in the healing process. The food scraps that we left behind were used to feed the hogs.

There was no such thing as saying we wanted to eat something different than what Mom had cooked. If you didn't eat what had been prepared, you weren't going to eat, so we learned to appreciate what we were given.

We repurposed items for reuse when we could. For example, when they bought flour it was in large cloth bags, they reused the cloth to make other items. To help keep us warm in the winter, my mom used flannel to make slips for us to wear under our clothes.

They collected S&H green stamps that were earned when they bought food. They used those stamps to buy dishes or glasses or other items offered by the stores.

We couldn't afford to go to the hairdresser; however, my mom knew how to press our hair and curl it. When she couldn't curl it, we were taught how to use either newspaper or strips from paper bags to wrap around our hair so we could get the curls we wanted. This actually worked really well.

We rarely went to the doctor because it was expensive. Home remedies were commonly used. Some of those remedies would be considered dangerous and unorthodox now, but they worked. Examples included a vinegar punch for antacid (vinegar, water, and baking soda); drinking teas made from corn husks and other items, some kind of candy like item made from coal oil/kerosene; using Epsom salt as a drink to "bring out" the measles; using milkweed plants for cuts, baking soda or salt was used in lieu of toothpaste, etc. Baking soda was also used in lieu of deodorant.

One of my cousins once stepped on some glass and a piece got stuck in her foot. When they couldn't remove it using a needle, my dad took a piece of salt meat and placed it on her foot and tied a rag around it. Somehow, it worked and a few hours later, the glass became visible and was able to be removed.

On the rare occasion we went to the doctor, I remember that blacks and whites had different waiting rooms and entrances to the office. I didn't understand why, but that was the way it was in the 60s and early 70s. Our elementary/junior high school was segregated, but by the time I went to high school, the schools were integrated. It was different, but we adjusted and were still able to excel. Several of us were high school valedictorians or salutatorians. I believe we all graduated with honors.

Find Joy Even In Hard Times

We worked hard and played even harder. Our creativity was also displayed during our play time because we often didn't have money for balls, bats, and other games, so we improvised. We would play soft ball with a rubber ball or with a ball that we made with rags. There weren't always enough people to make up a full team, so a person was "out" either when they were tagged with the ball or when someone threw and hit them with the ball before they got to the base. Sometimes the boys threw really hard. We played basketball, hide and seek and used our imagination when making mud cakes and using clay to make images. We used rocks to play jack rocks and often got splinters in our hands while playing jack rocks on the wood porches. We jumped rope, walked on an old barrel, played with a corn cob by placing a feather in it to see how far we could throw it, and we played hop scotch. We even rolled around in old tires while someone pushed us.

I'm sure our parents had worries and concerns about how they were going to provide, but we never saw the despair. There was joy in the midst of our hard times.

Prime the Pump

Before we had indoor plumbing, we had to pump water to be used for drinking, washing clothes, dishes, bathing, as well as for other uses. One of the things we always looked for when we went to the pump was a cup or bucket that already had water in it. We needed to pour that water into the pump in order to create enough pressure to bring up more water. Once we finished pumping our water, we were always required to leave some water in a bottle or a bucket so that the next person who needed to get water from the pump had the water necessary to prime it.

Lessons learned:

- Water for the pump is similar to a seed for the next crop. You have to invest something in order to get a return. In other words, you have to give in order to get. It's important to invest in things from which you expect to receive a return.
- Invest in your education if you want to receive knowledge.
- Invest in people in order for them to reach their potential.
- Invest your labor in order to receive funds to live on.
- Don't expect to receive a return, if you're not willing to "prime the pumps" in your life.

- If you invest only a little, only expect to receive a little in return.
- Leave something behind for the next person or next generation.

Develop an Excellent Work Ethic

We worked long hours doing manual labor. Our hands were sore and calloused, our skin was sunburned, but we had to work. We didn't know anything about sunscreen and even if we did, we couldn't afford it. We each wore a straw hat, a bandana to cover our hair, long sleeves, long pants, socks and closed toed shoes as protection from the sun and from other things in the fields – snakes, worms, bees, etc. That hard work became an incentive for us to strive to do better, to do well in school, and eventually to be able to work with our brains rather than with our hands.

Our parents would often say that because of our race, we needed to work twice as hard as everyone else in order to get ahead. Their expectation for us was excellence! We would be reprimanded if we didn't do things correctly. My dad sometimes cussed, and would say things like, "Don't s*** and step in it. Don't do things half-a**ed." In other words, do things right. Don't mess up, and if you do, don't make things worse.

Be smarter, work harder, and watch out for hidden traps. Dad would say something like, if you know that someone has set a trap for you, don't be a fool and walk into it.

Prepare for the Unexpected

Life happens. Unexpected things will happen, you just don't know when. Prepare for them.

Save for emergencies. Make it a priority to save for an emergency. Our parents didn't spend all the money they made during the summers or during the harvests. They put some money aside for emergencies and to help "tide them over" during the winter months. They always had a plan for their money. It may not have been a written budget, but daddy was good with numbers and knew how to keep track of where the money needed to be spent.

Shop wisely. Another part of being prepared was in how they shopped. If they found items at a good sale price, they would buy as much of that item that they could afford. They wanted to make sure that there was food to eat or other basic items available, if needed, during hard times.

Defend yourself. We grew up with guns in multiple rooms in the house. There was actually a rifle mounted on the wall over the bed I slept in. We were taught how to shoot and were told to never play with guns. Guns were used for two purposes: to hunt for food and for protection. Protection was necessary because of all the things that happened to black people in Mississippi. Unfortunately, even as I write this book, there are still injustices happening to black people in our country.

Know automobile basics. Learning to drive out in the country was rather easy. We didn't have a lot of traffic to contend with on the roads. We could always go down a dirt road to get more driving practice. Before we could get our drivers' license, daddy taught us how to check the oil and other fluid levels, put gas in the car, and how to change a tire. Those were deemed to be necessities, especially for us seven girls.

In those days there were no cell phones and we were taught not to hitchhike. Our parents wanted us to be able to take care of ourselves, so that we wouldn't have to be dependent on others to take care of us. My youngest sister said that she was always told to take the same route going to and from a location. That way, my dad would know where to start looking for her, if she didn't arrive home at the appointed time.

Tomorrow isn't promised. The folks in our neighborhood would usually end a promise with these sayings, "Lord willing or if the Lord is willing" or "If I live and nothing happens." I just thought it was a manner of speech, but now I know that they knew that they didn't control life and even our tomorrows are dependent upon the will of God. I think it was their way of acknowledging the sovereignty of God in our lives. Our very breath depends on Him.

No one looked forward to death, but we knew it happened. My first real recollection of death was on a stormy, rainy day. Usually, when it would thunder and lightning my mom would always tell us to "sit down and be quiet while the Lord does His work." Well, children being quiet with rain falling on the tin roof of the house, soon led to us taking a nap. We were awakened when the phone rang. I heard my dad say, "Ham's been struck by lightning." He then rushed out of the house. My dad's twin sister's husband was named Eddie, but everyone called him Hambone. We called him Uncle Ham. Hours passed and when dad returned he told us that Uncle Ham had been struck by lightning while he was driving home on the tractor. He was struck a short distance from home. The lightning also struck the clock and television in my aunt's house. The lightning strike and his fall from the tractor when he was struck led to his death. I recall hearing that all of his bones were broken.

There was a man who periodically came to the house to collect money. He would record the payment on a card and then give it to my parents. I later realized that this was the insurance man, and my parents were paying premiums for burial policies for all of us. These policies would pay a certain dollar amount to take care of funeral costs. I assume that my relatives had similar policies on their families. The premiums varied, depending on the number of people insured, but the payments were necessary. Funeral costs without those policies would have cost even more economic hardship.

Later in life, I spent over 30 years working in the field of insurance, and learned the value of preparing for the unexpected. Other types of insurance to consider based on your life's needs could include: life, long term care, auto, health, disability, homeowners, renters, flood, boat, motorcycle, commercial, business interruption, and earthquake insurance. Review your assets, protect what you value.

Value and Appreciate What You Have

Money was scarce and we didn't often get new things. I remember when my parents bought a new sofa and love seat. This was a major purchase, and the furniture had to last us for a long time. There was no such thing as changing out sofas every few years. In order to protect the furniture, it was covered in heavy plastic. We sat on the plastic, which was hot and sticky in the summers. Years later, after the plastic wore out, the sofa and love seat were always covered with sheets. The only times when the plastic or sheets were removed from the sofa were when we had guests from out of town.

Although our house wasn't modern and had many flaws, we were taught to always keep it clean. We would sweep, mop, and scrub the wood floors and keep everything clean. There was pride in keeping things clean.

Our parents always told us that "you can always find someone who wishes they had what you have, so be grateful and give thanks." They also said things like: "Being poor is no excuse for being dirty. Clean what you have and take care of it. Don't tear up those shoes, because that's all you've got."

Most of the time our parents would buy clothes for us and we had to wear what they purchased. If you didn't like what you were given, there was a good possibility that it would be taken from you and given to another sibling. Mom would also buy fabric for my sister and me to make clothes. We had to figure out how to make it work. When we were older, occasionally we were given the opportunity to shop with mom so that we could pick out clothes that we liked. This was a treat for us!

Actions Have Consequences Which Impact Others

We learned early that there was a difference between right and wrong. We also learned that consequences were associated with the choices we made. Some consequences were good; others were bad. Sometimes others will pay for the mistakes you make and sometimes they will receive the benefits from your choices. The bad consequences didn't feel good either.

We had situations in our house when something was broken, or misplaced, or missing and none of us children ever admitted to causing the item to be broken, misplacing an item or taking something that wasn't ours. Our parents knew that someone was guilty, they just didn't know who it was. There were a few times when we all received punishment for a bad deed because no one confessed to doing it. I never thought this was fair, but later in life, I came to realize that this principle holds true and applies to life today.

We've heard of numerous scandals that have shaken the business world, from ENRON to WorldCom to the most recent situation with Boeing. Ethics in the workplace has become situational and in some cases people don't believe in absolute rights and wrongs. Greed, lust for power, and sometimes bad decisions can lead to making wrong choices. Unfortunately, often many people are left to suffer the consequences of the actions of a few. It may not be fair that others are impacted, but it does happen. (Read Romans 5:8-21)

Consequences are not always bad. Sometimes, the decisions made by a few result in benefits for many. The seeds planted and lessons taught by our parents laid the foundation that we have built upon and has led to the success of our generation and for future generations. Jesus' death on the cross, provided a way for salvation for those who believe in Him and receive Him by faith. (Read Romans 5:8-21)

Set Expectations

Our parents set high expectations by planting a dream for a better life in our hearts. My dad always said that he wanted his children to have a better life than he had, so he always told us that education was the key. We were mandated to finish high school and strongly encouraged to go to college.

Simply going to school was not enough. Excellence was expected. Dad would attend parent teacher conferences and both parents would review our report cards each six weeks of the school terms.

Not only were we expected to excel in school, we were also expected to be respectful and obedient to our teachers as well as other adults. We knew that if a teacher had to discipline us, then that would really lead to more discipline at home by our parents. In those days corporal punishment was allowed in the schools; i.e. spankings with belts or paddles.

Looking back, I can see the wisdom in focusing on an education. They realized that there was more to life than working in the fields and barely getting by. They wanted us to succeed. Education gives knowledge, and knowledge becomes the key to unlocking opportunities. Doing well in school earned several of us academic scholarships which helped to pay for our education. We all graduated from high school, and all of us have been gainfully employed. Several of us are now retired. Seven of the nine children completed bachelors and master's degrees; one earned an associate's degree.

We in turn have set similar expectations with our children, who are also doing the same thing with their children.

Don't Allow Help to Become a Lifelong Crutch

The modern Supplemental Nutrition Assistance Program (SNAP) formally known as Food Stamps began as a pilot project in 1961 and was authorized as a permanent program in 1964. I'm not sure when we first starting getting food stamps, but I think I was still in elementary school. My parents had to go to the Food Stamp office which at that time did not include any people of color on staff. We would get food stamp booklets and also received "commodities" which included government cheese, peanut butter, powdered milk, a can of meat, and a few other things. It helped us for a short time.

I remember that my dad was not a fan of the program. He eventually told my mom that he was tired of going up to the Food Stamp Office to have "those people treat me as less than a man" because of all the questions they asked, so he withdrew from the program. To make ends meet, my dad started cleaning office buildings at night to make extra money. He worked in the fields during the day, came home, ate and then headed to town to work his second job. He often took some of us children with him to work so that he could finish the job sooner. We helped to empty the dirty ash trays, dusted and helped clean the break rooms and bathrooms. My twins tell me that when they visited during the summer, dad also let them help him clean offices.

Daddy even discouraged Momma from borrowing things like sugar or flour from her sister who lived across the road. However, mom would sometimes send one of us over to my aunt's house to borrow something. We became skillful in hiding the borrowed item so daddy wouldn't see it. We always repaid what we borrowed.

I remember that the other families in the neighborhood continued to get the food stamps. We didn't understand why we didn't get the free food, but now I believe that daddy made the right call. He didn't want to become dependent on the government for assistance as long as he could work. He was setting an example and teaching us a lesson about being independent. Ask for help when you need it, but don't let it become a lifelong crutch!

Plan, Till, Sow, Care, Reap/Harvest

Farm work required planning - when to plant, where to plant, how to plant, and what to plant. Our family watched the weather every day, used the Farmers' Almanac, and knew the seasons to determine when to plant.

They studied the land to determine what to plant and where to plant it. Certain areas of the land held more water than others so they avoided planting some items in those spots. Also they needed to periodically rotate the crops so the soil could be replenished. The primary crops that were planted were cotton, soybeans, and wheat. Prior to planting the seeds, the soil had to be tilled in order to help control weeds and to break up and loosen the soil so that the seeds could be planted.

Once the crops were planted, the farmers had to wait for sunshine and rain. They couldn't control the weather, but God could. So they had to trust God to do things only He could do so that the seeds would produce plants. Weeds also grew in the fields. When that occurred, we had to chop or pull the weeds so that it was easier for the plants to grow. This wasn't a "once and done" activity. It had to be done as needed. There were times when the fields were sprayed to get rid of bugs, grass, and weeds, so that they would not destroy the crops. Eventually the crops were harvested and sold; then the process started over.

Farming is similar to life. Lots of life lessons can be derived from this process. Jesus even gave a parable about the sower and the seed. (See the following chapters in the Bible: Matthew 13; Mark 4; and Luke 8)

- Just like seeds have the potential to bring forth crops, so do we. In order to reach our potential, we need to have a plan for our lives. Know the times and the seasons of life, and do what you've been called to do. Water the seeds with education, knowledge, faith, and work.
- Break up the ground to make it suitable to plant the seed. There are things in our lives that could hinder the gifts and talents we have from being fruitful. We have to till the soil of our hearts and habits. Once the seed is planted, cover that seed and water it with the Word of God, wisdom, knowledge, faith, and good works.
- You can't always see what is happening once you've planted the seed. You have to be patient, wait, and trust God. He's working even when we don't see, hear, or feel Him. "Now faith is the

substance of things hoped for, the evidence of things not seen." (Hebrews 11:1)

- Just as the farmer has to depend on God to cause the sun to shine, to give rain, and cause the seed to germinate and become a plant, we must depend on Him to help develop our talents and potential. Trust God to do what you can't do. We are dependent on God for favor, grace, mercy, salvation, deliverance and to show us the plans He has for us. He will work in us to bring forth fruit in our lives – if we let Him.

- Things in life will be like weeds to discourage you and prohibit your growth. Weeds must be removed or neutralized. This is a continual process. Eventually the crop will mature and you will reap the reward of your labor.

- Once you've accomplished one thing in life, it's time to start the process over again. Keep going, don't give up, there is always more work to do and more to accomplish.

- Not all seeds sprout in one season. Sometimes they show up years later. I remember seeing a few plants of corn in cotton fields, or vice-versa. These were from seeds that had been planted years earlier, but grew after the land was being used for a different purpose. Don't give up on your seeds. In due season, you will reap if you don't give up. (See Galatians 6:9 in the Bible)

Show Respect

We were taught to say, "Yes ma'am, and no ma'am, yes sir and no sir." Lying wasn't tolerated, especially to our parents. We were taught to ask each parent for permission to engage in activities, such as leaving the house, spending the night with cousins, going to games, etc. If we asked mom, she would always say, "Ask your daddy." He would do the same thing and tell us to "Ask your momma." Rather than going back and forth to each one of them, we finally learned to say, "Momma said yes, but I need to get your permission."

We had to respect teachers and other adults. Respecting authority included not interrupting adults while they were talking, not being loud or "sassy", and doing what we were told to do. Our parents rarely repeated a request/order. We knew that we needed to obey quickly. The good thing is that we were never obligated to do anything that was wrong.

We were also taught not to belittle other people, and not let people look down on or belittle us. People have value regardless of their position. We can learn something from almost anyone.

"Respect God. Don't take the Lord's name in vain. Respect the church and the house of God." These statements still resonate with me today.

Relationships – Be Careful Who You Associate With

Not everyone has your best interest at heart. Anytime my parents met a new person, they always asked the question: "Who are your people?" I often wondered why this was important. However, my parents felt it was important to know who we were associating and interacting with. They believed that the "fruit didn't fall far from the tree" and that a person's character often reflected the character of their parents and the people they associated with.

They tried to teach us that not everyone could be trusted. The phrase they would use when this happened was: "I don't trust him/her any further than I can throw them." This was a warning for us to be careful around that individual.

Another possible reason for asking this question was to determine if we were somehow related to the individual. Knowing a person's background and their relatives helped to assess if we were "kin" or not.

Your Word is Your Bond

Daddy would say, "Don't write a check that your a** can't cash." If you promise to do something, do it. Make sure it's legal. People should be able to count on your words. Don't promise something if you don't intend to keep that promise.

If you make a habit of breaking promises, your reputation will be negatively impacted. If you've proven that your word isn't worth the paper it's written on, then no one will trust you, extend you credit, or help you. On the contrary, if you keep your word, then, you will earn the trust of others.

If you make a bill, take out a loan, or borrow money, pay it back. If you can't pay it back, go to the person you owe and explain the situation to him/her and work out a repayment plan. Don't just ignore the person or try to hide from them.

Trust In and Wait On God

Mom would often sing a song that said, "You can't hurry God, no you have to wait. You have to trust Him and give Him time, no matter how long it takes. He's a God that you can't hurry. He'll be there, don't you worry. Although He may not come when you want Him, He's always right on time."

She trusted God's word and expected Him to fulfill it, even when people did wrong. It was reflective of Galatians 6:7-9, that reads: "Be not deceived; God is not mocked: for whatsoever a man soweth, that shall he also reap. For he that soweth to his flesh shall of the flesh reap corruption; but he that soweth to the Spirit shall of the Spirit reap life everlasting. And let us not be weary in well doing: for in due season we shall reap, if we faint not." God doesn't move in our timing, so we must trust Him, be patient, and wait for Him to move.

PART III: SEEDS OF FAITH

Seeds of Faith

From an early age I remember being awakened every Sunday morning by the radio playing gospel music and hearing my mom singing along while clapping her hands or patting her feet. We only had "church" with the preacher once a month, but on the 2nd Sunday when we met, we would get dressed and go to church. Mom and some of my aunts sang in the choir, and when I was older, I sang too. We also had weekly Sunday School classes.

Church clothes had to be clean and ironed because it was taboo to iron on a Sunday in our home. All of the ironing had to be done on Saturday or earlier in the week. Sunday was considered "the Lord's Day" and little work (other than cooking) was done. You wore your best to church. We were not allowed to chew gum in church, and we were encouraged to be on our best behavior. Our parents would often give us money to put in the collection plate – usually a few pennies, or a nickel when we had it, but we were taught to give.

Every year we had revival. During revival they always put chairs out front and anyone who wanted to know God more would come down front and pray and ask God to forgive their sins and ask Jesus into their hearts. This process was called being on the "mourning bench". During the time we were on the mourning bench, we were not supposed to play with other children, because we were being serious in seeking God. Our parents would tell us to not get up until we felt a change in our heart. Once that happened we would then become a candidate for baptism.

There were no swimming pools for us to be baptized in. We had a bayou. The banks of the bayou were overgrown with grass and weeds and someone had to mow the area with a tractor and disc plow to create a path for us to get to the water. We all wore white gowns and head coverings that our parents made for us to be baptized in. I remember the preacher and a deacon being in the water and beckoning for each candidate to come forward. It was muddy and I remember looking around to make sure there were no snakes in the water. Baptism went quickly and we rushed home to get cleansed, dried off, and got our hair styled before we went back to church to become an official member of the church.

I don't recall any bible studies at home or other overt biblical teachings other than Sunday School, and what we heard from the preacher. I didn't have my own Bible for a long time. While in high school, there was a group that passed out red copies of the New Testament that also included the books of Psalm and Proverbs.

I would see mom on her knees praying and she often prayed out loud. I only remember hearing my dad pray when we went to his church. I would hear the deacons and the preacher pray out loud. Their prayers had a rhyme and rhythm, and they were usually pretty repetitive.

Singing gospel songs and hymns occurred often at home and in the fields while we worked. Now that I have time to reflect on those songs, I realize how much faith and scriptural references were included in the songs. Although I didn't realize it then, I now know that the seed of faith had been planted and a foundation was being laid for my faith to be built upon. If I didn't learn anything else, I learned that God loved me and Jesus is the only one who can save me. Those songs conveyed messages of love, grace, mercy, hope, trust, patience, faith, and the blessing of salvation. Some of the songs taught us that there is a spiritual war going on for our souls, which requires us to fight – in the spirit.

Below are some examples of the songs I heard while growing up. I'm not sure if the titles are correct, but this is what I remember. I've grouped them according to the messages they taught and the seeds they planted.

Lessons in Songs

God Loves Us:

- Yes, Jesus Loves Me
- Jesus Loves the Little Children
- The Lord is Blessing Me Right Now

Sin is overcome by the Blood of Jesus and God's Grace

- Jesus Paid It All
- Amazing Grace
- Nothing But The Blood of Jesus
- I Know It Was The Blood
- What a Friend We Have In Jesus
- Search Me Lord
- Look Where He Brought Me From
- One Thing I Know, I've 'Sho' Been Born Again
- Near the Cross

Trust God and Find Hope in Him - God Is In Control

- I Will Trust in The Lord
- Hold to His Hand, God's Unchanging Hand
- There's a Brighter Day Ahead
- It's Just Another Day's Journey
- The Lord Will Make a Way Somehow
- Jesus Will Fix It For You
- I Need Thee Every Hour
- We've Come This Far by Faith
- Walk With Me Lord
- He's Got the Whole World In His Hands
- Wade In The Water
- Pass Me Not Oh Gentle Savior
- Where Could I Go But To The Lord

- I'm So Glad Trouble Don't Last Always
- Precious Lord Take My Hand

Have Patience

- You Can't Hurry God
- All of My Appointed Time

Death affects everyone – be prepared for it.

- I'm Going Home On The Morning Train
- Soon One Morning When Old Death Comes Creeping in My Room
- Will The Circle Be Unbroken
- Jordan River, I'm Bound To Cross
- Down By The Riverside
- I'll Be Somewhere Listening For My Name
- What A Time – When All God's Children Get Together

Hymns/Songs of Gratitude

- Thank You Lord
- This Morning When I Rose
- Look Where He Brought Me From
- Hymns: I love the Lord He heard my cry and pitied every groan. Long as I live while troubles rise, I'll hasten to His throne. Another hymn was Guide Me Oh Thou Great Jehovah

- "When I rose this morning, I said thank you Lord.....Ain't nothing but a savior brought me safe thus far."

Spiritual fight

- We Are Soldiers In The Army
- Joshua Fought The Battle of Jericho

PART IV: SEEDS OF LEGACY

Leave a Legacy

Prior to our parents' death, they were wise enough to have wills which outlined how they wanted their estate to be distributed. That was part of their financial legacy to us. Our parents weren't financially wealthy; however, they left us a legacy that's far greater than money or property. They taught us to believe in ourselves, work hard, play fair, trust in God, pursue excellence, and leave something of value behind for our loved ones.

We learned that there is hope in what should have been hopeless situations. There is joy even in sorrow. There is success in moving forward. Don't give up when the way gets tough. Remember, you're just building muscle and experiences to help prepare you for what lies ahead.

Despite the hardships of being poor sharecroppers, our parents planted and nourished some good seeds. None of us attended expensive Ivy League schools. Junior colleges and primarily Historically Black Colleges and Universities (HBCUs) provided a path for us to gain knowledge and move forward. Their nine children and 26 grandchildren have become: an inspector/registered sanitarian for a state, teachers (math, science, biology, elementary), office workers, supervisors, a Certified Public Accountant/Finance Director for a major city, an insurance executive, an author, a Lieutenant Colonel in the Army, computer programmers, government employees, a pharmacist, radiology technician, speech pathologist, occupational therapist, entrepreneur, retired NFL player, HVAC contractor, nurses, business analysts, claims representatives, underwriters, managers, accountants, engineers, division one (1) basketball player, a sailor and more. As of this writing, there are 21 great grandchildren who I believe will continue the journey.

What legacy are you leaving behind? Someone is watching you, listening to you, and may be modeling your behavior. You have the ability to either positively or negatively influence your family and people you know. Don't be afraid to encourage others to follow in your footsteps or to accomplish more than you were able to accomplish.

I pray that this book has illustrated that light cannot be hidden by the darkness of the past. Seeds sown and lessons taught will sprout in the right environment. So sow good seeds.

Our parents weren't perfect and neither are we. I encourage you to live the life you were created to live. We will make mistakes along the way. When we do, we must get up, keep the legacy alive, build on it, and leave a legacy for others to follow. I encourage you to make Jesus Christ the foundation for your legacy!